12 KEYS

TO
KINGDOM LIVING

Eric T. Roscoe

ISBN: 978-1-7355223-1-9

12 Keys to Kingdom Living is a spiritual life manual packed with spiritual truths that will teach believers how to engage in a relationship with our Heavenly Father and how to apply biblical principles in their life in order to receive desired results. In this manual, Eric T. Roscoe leads you on a journey through prophetic revelation by sharing 12 Kingdom principles he learned along his Christian walk in order to help you live a more productive life in God. As you take this journey, allow the Holy Spirit to lead and guide you in applying these principles in your personal walk with our Heavenly Father as you learn to prosper in every area of your life.

TABLE OF CONTENTS

Introduction

The best testimony to give is not always in how you got delivered. Sharing a testimony of how you are presently living a life that reflects your deliverance and the light of God, would cause someone to become attracted to the light you carry. They will have the opportunity to see and believe in God through you

I have been through a lot in my short time on the Earth and in the Kingdom of God, but I thank the Lord for every moment----He allowed it all to work for my good. I have come to encourage you: He is allowing everything you have been through to work for your good as well. On my journey with the Lord, I have learned how to enjoy life, and my relationships more intentionally by living by three L's:

Live *intentionally* and on *purpose.*

Love *without measure* through disappointments, pain, and despite the offenses of others.

Learn by using everything life throws you as *an opportunity* to learn and grow from your mistakes as well as from others.

2

Use every adversity and mistake as a stepping-stone to victory. By doing so, your life will testify of the power and grace of God, allowing people to see and experience Him through you. What you say, you believe! Doing this and continuing to learn of the Lord's characteristics, His will, nature, and benefits will help you cultivate and produce the fruit of the Spirit in your life. All these things are void and impossible without receiving salvation, deliverance, and the baptism of the Holy Spirit!

The Greek word for salvation is *sótéria*
Transliteration: *sótéria*
Phonetic Spelling: (*so-tay-ree'-ah*)
Definition: welfare, prosperity, deliverance, preservation, salvation, safety.

Salvation is a gift and the doorway into the Kingdom. One receives salvation by accepting Christ in their heart as their Lord and Savior. A person can be born again, but they may still need deliverance in certain areas. Salvation is another name for deliverance, but it means to be delivered spiritually or to be saved (born again). Deliverance is one of the benefits of receiving salvation and is initially done spiritually, but must be continued as we walk with the Lord. As we continue to walk with Him, we receive deliverance from the snares of the enemy. The Lord has delivered me from things instantly and other times, there was a process I had to endure for the deliverance to take place.

There is a distinct difference between water baptism and the baptism of the Holy Spirit. Water baptism is an outward expression of an inward change. It is done as a sign of belief and symbolizes that you have died and been resurrected just like Christ. The baptism of the Holy Spirit is when you are immersed in the life of the Spirit, and He begins to have more influence over you and in you. This is important because in Acts 1:8, Jesus said you will "receive power after the Holy Ghost comes upon you." Not only to do what He did, but so we can live like He lived, allowing the life of God and fruit of the Spirit to flow through us! In Luke 17:21, He began to talk about the Kingdom of God, and He said it does not come with observations meaning you will not be able to say it is here or there because the Kingdom of God is within you! In other words, when we receive the Holy Spirit, we receive everything that is in the Kingdom. The task then becomes learning how to allow the Kingdom to flow out of you. You may ask yourself how this is possible. I have great news! It is not easy, but it is not hard either. God is just as committed as you are. If you are willing to remain disciplined and committed, you are on your way.

1

NEW MAN, NEW MIND

The mistake made by many is helping people to get saved, but not teaching and training them as disciples. As a result, they are set up for inevitable failure. We must help people understand salvation happens spiritually first, but must be worked out naturally. It starts with accepting Jesus Christ into your heart and receiving the Holy Spirit which regenerates your spirit that was once dead. Then, we must discover our new identity. To embrace this new life and new experiences, we must get new information, a revelation about our new life, and renew our mind. Romans 12:2 teaches us: "Be not conformed to the world, but be transformed by the renewing of our mind so you may prove what is the good, acceptable, and perfect will of God." The issue now becomes, our Spirit has been saved but not the soul and the body. We are a three-part being: spirit, soul, and body. Salvation must be worked out in each part. There are many processes to undergo during a Christian journey. A process of deliverance, a process of healing, a process of repentance, and a process of sanctification, just to name a few. As believers, we are constantly being delivered and healed from old thought patterns, habits, and behaviors. These are called strong-holds; A stronghold is a pattern of thinking connected to a belief system that fosters your current perception to reality. There are both Godly and demonic strongholds, depending on which ideas concerning your life you decide to embrace. This becomes an issue as a believer if what you perceive about yourself as reality is according to the old nature and the lies of Satan that opposes the truth God desires to reveal. Your mind must align to the new regenerated nature within you that you have become in Christ. This is known as repentance.

There are two Hebrew words for repentance which are *nacham* and *shub*. Nacham means to lament or to grieve. These are emotions that are aroused when motivated to take a different course of action. *Shub* means to have a radical change of mind toward sin. This change implies a conscious moral separation from sin to decide to forsake it and agree with God. On this journey, the understanding of repentance will need to be embraced for success and continual progression. The process of repentance is incorporated into our lifestyle.

The Greek word for repentance is *metanoia* which literally means to have another mind or change your mind about something. The process of sanctification is both spiritual and natural. The word sanctify means to set apart.

For God to begin the renovation process within us, He must set us apart from people, places, and things that can potentially hold us back or distract us from moving in a new direction with Him. Everyone is not strong enough to stay around the things they are held captive to while doing the work for their new life. It is a process in which we must learn to separate from one way of thinking and being and conform to His way. In Apostle Paul's writing to the church, he said we are a slave to whomever we obey, whether it be the flesh or the Spirit. The body is a slave to the soul, and the soul is our mind, will, and emotions. The soul is made up of everything we have learned and experienced prior to salvation, so now we must unlearn some doings and be taught some new ways. As we renew our minds as Roman 12:2 teaches, we must "pray and yield to the Holy Spirit." We begin to be transformed more and more as the enemy loses power in our lives. Transformation will not stop attacks, but you will rise to a place where you are able to stand against all opposition through the Word and exercise your dominion and authority. As you begin the process of allowing God to give you a new mind, you will begin to create a new life. Everyone and everything around you will appear differently. Over time, He will begin to reveal things about your purpose and why you were created. You will realize God has always been a part of your life, and that He has watched over you even when you were not aware. He will take you from faith to faith and glory to glory. Another part of this process is learning to commune with the Holy Spirit and how to allow Him to express Himself through you. This process will be felt and measured through any of the following fruit of the Spirit: love, joy, peace, patience, goodness, meekness, gentleness, and self-control. Use this to measure your own personal growth and development in the spirit. You will find that as you mature and learn to yield to the Holy Spirit, these fruit will be a by product of your submission.

These are the Instructions I believe will help you:

1. *Read all three Gospels* to learn about the life of Jesus and understand the nature and character of God expressed through Him. He only did what His Father told Him to do and what He saw the Father doing. Jesus lived a life

committed to God the father and the communion of the Holy Spirit. Because of his radical obedience, we get to experience his love through salvation, deliverance, and miracles. All of this from the result of this commitment and intimate relationship with God.

2. *Read all the letters Paul wrote to the New Testament churches* as instructions for Godly living while allowing the Holy Spirit to be your guide.

3. *Create a sanctuary and altar for yourself.* Cultivate an environment of worship and the Word, whether you are driving, in the shower, in the office, or watching TV. The more you feed the Word to your spirit, the easier it becomes to manage your thought life. Your altar is the place where you meet with God, and constantly lay down your life to receive His.

4. **Extra study:** Galatians 2:20, 1 Corinthians 2:16, Philippians 2:5-8, and Romans 8:29.

<u>Pray this Prayer:</u>

Heavenly Father,
I thank you that I have been crucified with Christ.
No longer do I live, but Christ lives in me. And the
life I live, I live by faith in the Son of God who died

for me and gave Himself. Father, I thank you that I have the mind of Christ. Thank you for allowing me to be conformed into His image in heart, mind, and obedience. Therefore, I die daily that He may live in me and through me. In Jesus' name, Amen.

2

APPLICATION GIVES BIRTH TO MANIFESTATION

In this lesson, we will discuss faith and the power of activating your faith. We have all heard the phrase, "Knowledge is power." I challenge that phrase by saying: "Knowledge produces power only when received, believed, and applied." Do you remember in the last lesson I stated, 'God will take us from glory to glory?' As we journey with the Lord, we grow in our intimacy with Him which ultimately determines how we view Him and ourselves. New believers are children of God, but handled differently due to the need to be taught by a shepherd that He sends to guide and teach them. When new believers mature in the faith and learn to be codependent upon the Holy Spirit, they are considered "Sons of God". Romans 8:14 KJV states, "those who are led by the Spirit of God are Sons of God." Therefore, there is a distinction.

As you continue to get to know your Heavenly Father as well as He knows you, He will begin to share secret things with you because you have become a friend of God. He knows He can trust you; it is His desire to share His heart and plans with His friends. Afterall, we are considered co-laborers with God in Christ (1 Corinthians 3:9). There are many scriptures we see in operation of this. In John 15:15, after the 12 disciples had been walking with Jesus for a while, Jesus says, *"I no longer call you servants because a servant does not know what his master's business is. Instead, I have called you friends."* Right before that in John 15:14, He says, *"You are my friends if you do what I command you."* There are different levels of intimacy and trust with God. This is the reason it is so important to understand God from a relational aspect, not just as the creator of the world. God wants us to live out what we believe. Hebrews 11:6 KJV reads, *"Without faith it is impossible to please God because whoever comes to him must believe that he is (God) and that he is a rewarder of them that diligently seek him."* To diligently seek means to consistently and intentionally be in pursuit of. The same way we got saved is the same way we must live—by faith.

In James 2:14-26, James wrote a whole chapter about how "faith without works is dead," meaning if it is not expressed through words and seen through actions, it will not work. Faith must be voice activated and moving. It is not enough to say what you believe without demonstrating that you believe in faith. Not only does it show God our level of faith, it allows others to see it as well.

These are the instructions I have for you:

1. *Be honest with yourself and with God* about where you are in your faith walk and where you desire to be.

2. *Identify your strong areas* of faith and see manifestation of it. Allow that to encourage you and push you forward.

3. *Write down the areas* where you recognize you are weaker in your faith (finances, peace, wisdom, confidence, fear, worry, unbelief, etc.) and find scriptures pertaining to those areas. Mediate, pray, and make declarations over yourself. Practice exercising the Word until the Lord leads you to move on to something else or when you know you believe it and can move on.

4. *Keep a journal* of your progression and the prayers you have before the Lord. Mark them off as you see the Lord cause it to come to pass.

5. *Extra study:* James 1: 22-25

Pray this Prayer:

Heavenly Father,
I thank you that I am a doer of your word and not just a hearer. I thank you for giving me faith to believe you at your word and the courage to walk in it. I receive your wisdom, understanding, and instructions concerning my life to be led by you and not of myself. Your word says in Proverbs 14:12, there is a way that seems right, but the end of that way is destruction. Father, I thank you for not allowing me to go that way but leading me in the way I am to go and the decisions I am to make. Holy Spirit, teach me, guide me, and direct me into all truth. In Jesus' name, Amen.

3

MAINTAINING A LIFE OF PEACE

Isaiah 26:3 NKJV encourages, "He will keep him in perfect peace whose mind is stayed on him." The measure of peace you experience is contingent on the measure of intentional thought and attention you give to Him as it concerns your life. Some years ago, my ex-wife told me she was not happy. The Holy Spirit prompted me to ask her a question. I asked, "Is it that you're not happy or you don't have peace?" She replied, "Both. If I was happy, I would have peace." So, the Lord allowed me to know she had not received His peace which is eternal and internal, and I could not give that to her. I tried explaining that to her and encouraging her to seek the Lord concerning His peace, but she chose not to. Living for 26 years with no peace, and finally receiving it in Him, I understood its value. Therefore, I was willing to guard, protect, and keep it at any means necessary. Even if it meant I had to learn how to guard my heart and control my tongue because the value is costly. I will share more about this subject in a later lesson.

The absence of a relationship with God, and a lack of intimacy with the Holy Spirit, causes one to not experience His peace. These things are given as a gift, another benefit of salvation. When a person does not have that connection with God, they put unnecessary pressure on someone else to give them what only their creator can. They believe another man or woman will provide them happiness and peace. The danger is when any of these things leave, so will their peace and happiness because these things are temporal, in essence. If your happiness is based on any of these things, it will be conditional. It also means that someone or something controls your peace and ability to be happy.

What is happiness? Happiness is a mental or emotional state of wellbeing, characterized by positive and pleasant emotions. If we are mentally or emotionally unstable, we will not be happy. Being happy is contingent on how you may feel or what is happening. Being mentally or emotionally unstable is when we operate out of our flesh, mind, will, and emotions that are not yielded to God. Mental and emotional stability comes when we connect and believe in the Word of God. Doing so allows Him to transform us through the renewing of our minds and help from the Holy Spirit. I struggled with this once upon a time, but when I heard televangelist Joyce Myers say we can learn how to enjoy the good ones and manage the bad, it shifted my mind and helped me to realize I had control over my mental and emotional state. God never intended for them to control me. The Holy Ghost began to take me to scriptures that validated my newfound revelation. I needed patience and self-control and they were both fruit of the Spirit that the Lord wanted to cultivate in me. So, I began to mediate and practice through my experiences and relationships with other people. Nothing happened overnight. I still messed up and made mistakes, but I eventually got better at exercising self-control by not reacting and responding out of my feelings. By being slow to speak, I learned everything does not require a response and reaction.

Proverbs 16:32 KJV reads, *"He that is slow to anger is better than the mighty; and he that ruleth his spirit than he that taketh a city."* James 1:19 KJV reads, *"Wherefore, my beloved brethren, let every man be swift to hear, slow to speak, slow to wrath."* Proverbs 19:11 NIV reads, *"A person's wisdom yields patience; it is to one's glory to overlook an offense."* Proverbs 25:28 NIV reads, *"Like a city whose walls are broken through is a person who lacks self-control."* Feelings and emotions constantly change. Living by emotions is dangerous and being unstable is even more dangerous. Seek God for eternal peace and stop blaming others for your lack of it. The reality is we must first be happy with ourselves as we begin to like ourselves more and appreciate the work God is doing in us. Learn to give everything to Him and not allow things to worry you and weigh you down. We can maintain the peace. He has given us a life of victory against every demonic attack.

What is peace? Peace is the quietness and tranquility in the soul and spirit. It is freedom from disturbance from outside influence. In other words, to be spiritually, mentally, and emotionally sound. It does not mean things around you are not disturbing. It just means inwardly you are unbothered and unshaken in your spirit. Peace is one of the gifts and fruits of the Spirit that Jesus gave to those who believed in Him before going back to the Father. Peace comes by virtue of receiving the Holy Spirit. John 14:26-27 AMP reads, *"But the Helper (Comforter, Advocate, Intercessor — Counselor, Strengthener, Standby), the Holy Spirit, whom the Father will send in My name [in My place, to represent Me and act on My behalf], He will teach you all things. And He will help you remember everything that I have told you. Peace I leave with you; My [perfect] peace I give to you; not as the world gives do I give to you. Do not let your heart be troubled, nor let it be afraid. [Let My perfect peace calm you in every circumstance and give you courage and strength for every challenge.]"* Romans 14:17 AMP reads, *"For the kingdom of God is not a matter of eating and drinking [what one likes], but of righteousness and peace and joy in the Holy Spirit."* Luke 17:20-21 AMP reads, *"Now having been asked by the Pharisees when the kingdom of God would come, He replied, "The kingdom of God is not coming with signs to be observed or with a visible display; 21 nor will people say, 'Look! Here it is!' or, 'There it is!' For the kingdom of God is among you [because of My presence]."*

Having the peace of God does not exempt us from going through things, it only promises to keep us as we go through trials and tribulations. When everything around us goes crashing down, we are still able to stand in peace. In 2 Corinthians 4:7-9 NKJV, The Apostle Paul said *"Now we have this treasure in earthen vessels, that the excellency of the power may be of God and not of us. We are troubled on every side, yet not distressed; we are perplexed but not in despair, persecuted, but not forsaken; cast down, but not destroyed."* This is a great depiction of the peace of God. It is His power and ability working on the inside of us keeping us together. Praise God! Peace is a choice. You are in control of allowing your peace to be disturbed by experiences, circumstances, and people. Yes, he comes to steal, kill, and destroy everything God has for us (John 10:10. It is up to us to protect our peace against the wiles and fiery darts of the enemy. There are many scripture references as it pertains to the peace of God. I encourage you to meditate on whichever one of these scriptures the Holy Spirit highlights to you and allow it to penetrate your heart to receive the benefit of His peace by faith. I have listed just a few below to assist.

Galatians 5:22-23 NIV reads, *"But the fruit of the Spirit is love, joy, peace, forbearance, kindness, goodness, faithfulness, gentleness and self-control. Against such things there is no law."*

John 16:33 NIV reads, *"I have told you these things, so that in me you may have peace. In this world you will have trouble. But take heart! I have overcome the world."*

Colossians 3:15 NIV reads, *"Let the peace of God rule in your hearts, since as members of one body you were called to peace. And be thankful."*

Hebrews 12:14 NIV reads, *"Make every effort to live in peace with everyone and be holy; without holiness no one will see the Lord."*

1 Peter 5:7 NIV reads, *"Cast all your anxiety on him, because he cares for you."*

These instructions will show you how to guard your peace:

> 1. **Understand the battle is not against people** (flesh and blood), but demonic spirits working through people (principalities, powers, and spiritual wickedness in high places). The Apostle Paul said we are not to be ignorant of his devices therefore we must be informed of what he is doing and who he uses to come against us.

> 2. *Guard your heart!* Proverbs 4:23 teach us to guard our hearts above all else because out of it flows the issues of life. In Luke 6:45, Jesus gives us more understanding by saying from the abundance of the heart the mouth speaks. In other words, if offense, anger, bitterness, or unforgiveness gets in our hearts, it will come out through our speech. This includes our negative thoughts and desires according to Matthew 15:19 and Mark 7:21. Our

speech reveals the current condition of our heart and whether we believe what God has spoken.

3. *Read Matthew 6:31 & the parable of the Sower in Luke 8:4-15.* There is much revelation locked in this parable for the Holy Spirit to unfold to you.

4. *After the Holy Spirit reveals to you where you are,* continue to be honest with yourself and the Lord. Allow the Holy Spirit to deal with you so He can mature you and perfect those things concerning you.

5. *Be intentional* about who you engage and commit to in relationships. There are relationships ordained by God to allow you to experience the peace of God and bring out the best version of yourself. Then, there are relationships assigned by the enemy to distract us and disturb our peace. We are even faulted with creating relationships on our own that may hinder our walk with God and journey to peace. This is the reason it is important to be sensitive to the Holy Spirit when engaging in relationships.

6. *Find a church or community of believers* that understand, teach, and demonstrate the fruits and gifts of the Spirit. As believers, we need to be in a culture that will bring out the Christ in us. To thrive, that environment needs to be saturated with the love of God, not religious spirits who are hypocritical and judgmental.

7. *Extra study*: John 14:16, John 15:26, Acts 2:33, 1 Corinthians 2:10 Peter 5:7, Isaiah 26:3, and Proverbs 3:5-6.

Pray this Prayer:

Heavenly Father,
You said in Philippians 4:6-7 to be anxious for nothing, but through prayer and supplication with thanksgiving to let our requests be known to you and the peace of God that passes all understanding shall guard our mind and hearts through Christ Jesus. Therefore, we cast all our cares unto you because we know you care for us. You said you would keep us in perfect peace whose mind stayed on you, therefore I lean not to my own understanding, but I acknowledge you in all my ways and trust you with all my heart and mind. Lead me in all your ways by

the Word and by your spirit in Jesus' name! Father, I thank you for your peace and I receive it by faith! Amen.

4

DEVELOPING PATIENCE IN THE STORMS OF LIFE

My favorite scripture on this subject matter is in the book of James 1:2-8. These verses have gotten me through many storms and transitions in my life. It states, *"My brethren, count it all joy when ye fall into divers temptation; knowing that the trying of your faith worketh patience. But let patience have her perfect work, that ye May be perfect and entire, wanting nothing. If any man lack wisdom, let him ask of God that gives to all men liberally, and upbraideth not, and it shall be given unto him. But let him ask in faith, nothing wavering. For he that wavereth is like a wave of the sea driven with the wind and tossed. For let not that man think that he shall receive anything of the Lord. A double minded man is unstable in all his ways."* The Apostle James, a disciple of Jesus under the influence of the Holy Spirit, encourages believers to be joyful when going through the storms of life and temptations placed before us, but we are to know these three things:

1. The trying of your faith is working and producing your personal patience and

trust in the Lord.

2. The trials and tests are molding and shaping your character, while also building your faith.

3. If we lack wisdom and understanding concerning the process, we should ask for wisdom and he will give it to us freely, but it must be received by faith and not doubt because doubt prevents us from receiving from the Lord.

Here are some scripture references that validate what the Apostle James stated in James 1-2:8. In 2 Thessalonians 1:4-5, Paul informs the church of Thessalonica how the Lord was excited about their perseverance and faith during the persecutions and trials they endured, and how as a result that has qualified them to be counted worthy of the Kingdom of God. Romans 5:3-4 NIV reads, *"Not only so, but we also glory in our sufferings, because we know that suffering produces perseverance; 4 perseverance, character; and character, hope."* James 1:12 NIV reads, *"Blessed is the one who perseveres under trial because, having stood the test, that person will receive the crown of life that the Lord has promised to those who love him.* Ephesians 6:18 AMP reads, *"With all prayer and petition pray [with specific requests] at all times [on every occasion and in every season] in the Spirit, and with this in view, stay alert with all perseverance and petition [interceding in prayer] for all God's people."* Galatians 6:9 AMPC reads, *"And let us not lose heart and grow weary and faint in acting nobly and doing right, for in due time and at the appointed season we shall reap, if we do not loosen and relax our courage and faint."* 2 Peter 1:5-6 NIV reads, *"For this very reason, make every effort to add to your faith goodness; and to goodness, knowledge; 6 and to knowledge, self-control; and to self-control, perseverance; and to perseverance, godliness..."*

Some ways that will help develop patience:

1. *Developing intimacy with the Lord* through prayer and worship will teach you how to wait on the Lord in confident trust.

2. *Mediate and invest* in learning the scriptures that apply to certain aspects of your life experiences and circumstances.

3. *Allow patience* to have its perfect work in you through experiences, trials, and tests so the Lord can perfect those things concerning you.

4. *Keep your supplications and petitions* before the Lord through prayer, confessions, and declarations.

5. *Pray often in the spirit* (in tongues) and in your understanding. Building your most holy faith will increase your sensitivity and give boldness in the things of God. I have learned praying the Word is one the most powerful and effective ways to pray as well as praying by the leading of the Holy Spirit.

6. *Guard your heart and protect your thoughts* from offense, doubt, fear, unbelief, and distractions. These things are designed by the enemy to steal your peace and rob your joy which will cause you to waver in your faith and cause you to speak and make decisions based on how you feel and not what God said.

7. *Extra study*: Mark 11:24 and James 1:5-6.

Pray this Prayer:

Heavenly Father,
You said in James 1:2-4 to count it all joy when we encounter trials of many kinds because the trying of our faith produces patience. You said let patience have its perfect work in us so that we can be perfected and matured in action, thought, and in deed. Therefore, I thank you for expanding my capacity to endure and to receive hardship. I thank you for expanding my capacity to receive what I'm supposed to learn from this situation. By faith, I receive the answers I seek. You said if I lack wisdom to ask, therefore I ask for wisdom concerning the area of peace. I receive it by faith in Jesus' name! Amen.

5

EMBRACING THE LOVE OF GOD

I believe one of the most important attributes to have as a Christian believer is the love of God. Receiving revelation concerning the length, depth, and height of His love is literally life changing for those that receive and reciprocate it back in their earthly relationships. God demonstrated His love by preparing a plan of salvation, redemption, and reconciliation through His son Jesus Christ. In this love, we see the expression of sacrificial giving. The Father gave us his son; the son laid down his life for his friends and in obedience to the Father, as a blood offering for the benefit of so many others that would come after him.

Love allows you to see past anyone's past or current condition to their God given purpose and potential. Love must be reciprocated for it to be beneficial. Yes, we know God loves us, and we say we love Him, but until it is fully received, love cannot be mirrored or reciprocated. I find it interesting that many people in the body of Christ do not understand

His love. Proof of this is being unable to demonstrate it. One can communicate His mind (His Word), but may not be able to communicate His heart, and demonstrate His love. There is a process within receiving and walking in the love of God because there are many depths and dimensions to His love that can only be mirrored by revelation, experience, and understanding.

Take a look at your personal relationships and analyze how people treat you, talk to you, and see you. It will reveal their level of capacity to love. I have come to know that a person cannot give you what they have not received. Therefore, if they have not received the love of God for themselves, they will not be able to give it to others. This releases the weight of the responsibility and allows those expectations to diminish.

Prior to my salvation, I did not like myself because of all I had done. However, there was someone who still loved me without it being measured by what I did or did not do. I learned God loved me because of His own purpose and intent for me. The more I received revelation about the character of God and His love for me, the more I was able to love myself and reciprocate that love to others. His love captured me, His grace captivated me, and His mercy saved me. I am His and there is nothing anyone can do or say about it. This amazing truth will liberate you from guilt, shame, and condemnation. You will better understand how your life has been pre-determined and predestined once you embrace the truth of God's love.

We cannot discuss love without discussing mercy. Mercy is when you choose to show compassion and forgiveness to someone when you hold the power to judge and cast stones at them. Instead, you give them an opportunity to repent and correct their wrongdoing. This is also how God deals with humanity. God does not run out of mercy like we do. In fact, *"His mercy is made new every morning day by day."* God wants us to adopt His mind, heart, and nature, but first we must let go of our old way of thinking and being. As He reveals Himself to us in new ways, we must learn to adjust ourselves to the truth He reveals. Extending mercy is not an excuse to allow people to treat you anyway and stay in relationships that are not purposeful. Mercy is simply a heart check and posture. We must walk in wisdom as it pertains to engaging in relationships. Every relationship sent to us is not from God, so it requires a keen spirit of discernment to help us navigate.

Here are just a few scriptures on the mercies of God that reveal the heart and mind of God: Hebrews 8:12 KJV reads, *"For I will be merciful to their unrighteousness, and their sins and their iniquities will I remember no more."* Titus 3:5 NIV reads, *"...he saved us, not because of righteous things we had done, but because of his mercy. He saved us through the washing of rebirth and renewal by the Holy Spirit..."* Psalm 145:8-9 AMP reads, *"The Lord is gracious and full of compassion, slow to anger and abounding in loving kindness. The Lord is good to all, And His tender mercies are over all His works [the entirety of things created]."* Ephesians 2:4 KJV reads, *"But God, who is rich in mercy, for his great love wherewith he loved us, Even when we were dead in sins, hath quickened us together with Christ, (by grace ye are saved) ..."*

The Father, in His great love and pursuit of humanity, chose to wink at all wrongdoing and decided to see the best in us through the blood of Jesus. I call this "The Great Exchange." I believe we will see great revival when we begin to understand this revelation because it will inspire people to preach the Gospel to those who may not know that God has forgiven them. If faith comes by hearing and hearing the word of God, then how can someone hear without a preacher proclaiming and explaining the finished works of Jesus Christ? It truly reflects the love of God and our love for Him and what He loves. Romans 5:5 KJV reads, *"And hope maketh not ashamed; because the love of God is shed abroad in our hearts by the Holy Ghost which is given unto us."*

Pray this Prayer:

Father,
I thank you that the love of God had been shed abroad in my heart by the Holy Spirit. Holy Spirit, teach me how to love in word, in truth, and in deed. Teach me how to be a good steward of your love and how to guard my heart with all diligence that nothing hinders my ability to receive your love and distribute it according to your loving kindness, mercy, and grace in Jesus' name! Amen.

6

THE LAW OF RECIPROCITY

Did you know the natural world is governed in the same way the spiritual world is governed? Well, it is. For instance, in the natural world, one of Sir Isaac Newton's Laws of Gravity teaches us "what goes up must come down." In the spiritual realm, this law correlates with the Law of Reciprocity, also known as *sowing and reaping*. In the Law of Reciprocity, whatever you do to others will be done to you. The Bible teaches this, and the world understands it, but it is known as *karma*. This concept is a spiritual principle we must understand to prosper in any area of life. For instance, who goes to the bank and attempts to make a withdrawal of a thousand dollars that has not been deposited into the account? You can only expect a return of what you have invested. We are to have the same understanding when it comes to what we receive from the Earth and God.

Whatever seed you sow today, you will eventually see in your tomorrow. If you know you are in need of love, sow love to others. If you know you will need forgiveness, mercy, and grace, sow that as well. Oftentimes, we think we are getting away with our actions, but the truth is it always shows up sooner or later because of this law. The foundational text for this principle is found in a few places in scripture: The first scripture addresses the law of time which God put in the Earth to govern time, seasons, and climates. Genesis 8:22 NIV reads, *"As long as the earth remains, seed time and harvest, cold and heat, summer and winter, and day and night will never cease."*

The following scriptures addresses mankind on several subjects and further explains *sowing and reaping*. It allows us to know we are responsible for the decisions we make, the words we speak, and how we decide to live our lives. Galatians 6:7 KJV reads, *"Be not deceived; God is not mocked: whatsoever a man sows, that shall he also reap."* Romans 2:6 NIV reads, *"God will repay each person according to what they have done."* 2 Corinthians 5:10 NIV reads, *"For we must all appear before the judgment seat of Christ, so that each of us may receive what is due us for the things done while in the body, whether good or bad."* Proverbs 18:21 NIV reads, *"The tongue has the power of life and death, and those who love it will eat its fruit.*

The next Law of Reciprocity principle I will share has to do with seed in monetary form. Scripture says, "God gives seed to Sower." If a person is selfish and reluctant to give, they may experience many dry seasons due to not participating with the law. Another part of this law states, "Give and it will be given to you." You do not have to give in seed form to reap monetarily. Sometimes, as we sow our time, resources, heart, and love, God places us on someone's heart to sow back in the form of gifts and money. It all starts with the first seed of the Sower. The same measure you give is the measure that will be measured back to you. We have no right to expect a return where we have not sown. The kingdom of darkness loves to play on our ignorance and blind spots, but God is releasing truth which shines His light into every dark place in your understanding. I prophecy the eyes of our understanding are being enlightened right now, in Jesus' name! Luke 6:38 ESV *reads, "Give, and it will be given to you. Good measure, pressed down, shaken together, running over, will be put into your lap. For with the measure you use it will be measured back to you."*

The last principle in the Law of Reciprocity is one of the most important principles because it addresses our eternal state. This is the Law of Love and Forgiveness, which states "You must forgive to be forgiven by the Father." Although we are forgiven through Jesus, a person choosing unforgiveness is choosing not to embrace the finished works on the Cross and the love of God that is expected to be reciprocated. Forgiveness sets not only the one offended free, but the offender as well. If a person never learns how to abide by the law of love, and passes the ultimate test of forgiving, they will not be able to receive forgiveness. Mark 11:25 NIV reads, *"And when you stand praying, if you hold anything against anyone, forgive them, so that your Father in heaven may forgive you your sins."* Matthew 6:14-15 ESV reads, *"...but if you do not forgive others their trespasses, neither will your Father forgive your trespasses."*

In conclusion, not only is it against the law not to love and forgive others for anyone considered to be a believer, but it is also a commandment that requires you to use your faith. God understands this may be a bit harder for some of you which is the reason He has given us grace which requires faith. Forgiveness is an act of faith but also an expression of love. We cannot do it in our own strength and ability; therefore, we lean into Him for help. Romans 14:23 AMP reads, *"But he who is uncertain [about eating a particular thing] is condemned if he eats, because he is not acting from faith. Whatever is not from faith is sin [whatever is done with doubt is sinful].*" John 13:34 ESV reads, "*A new commandment I give to you that you love one another, just as I have loved you, you are also love one another.*"

I encourage all my brothers and sisters in the Kingdom to study this law and exercise it in their life. It will bless you tremendously, and God will be pleased. For some people forgiveness is hard, but the truth is forgiveness is a decision. Once we embrace the truth that we have been forgiven, it will be hard not to forgive others when God has freely forgiven you.

If you are finding it difficult in your heart to forgive, pray:

Heavenly Father,
Thank you for your son Jesus who was delivered for our trespasses and raised for our justification. Your word says to forgive so that I can be forgiven, therefore I repent and forgive _____ for what they have done to me. I release all pain, guilt, and shame of past relationships and I receive a new heart, a new mind, and a new life. I declare I have the mind of Christ and Christ forgives. I renounce hurt, rejection, and fear of rejection, abuse, and torment in Jesus' name and I declare I am forgiven because I choose to forgive. In Jesus' name, Amen!

7

IDENTITY REVEALS PURPOSE

When I did not know who I was or my purpose, I wasted a lot of time doing things that were unproductive, sowing to my flesh. I was merely existing, not yet living. I discovered the reason for my existence when I connected to the Life Giver and became born again. After getting saved, I received more of a sense of purpose although I didn't quite understand what that purpose was. The Lord showed me how many people in the body of Christ have been out of alignment because they were unaware of their identity and purpose. Of course, this is one of the many reasons prophetic teachers are arising like never before. In order to help the body grow in more understanding, and unlock revelation within them.

Many have been out of place — out of divine alignment in Consequence. As a result, the enemy has played on our ignorance, causing us to be ineffective believers and witnesses for the Kingdom. I believe God is changing that as you read these words. I believe when the focus of having and going to church changes to teaching believers to become more aware that they *are* the church, the culture will shift. Meaning, we shall go from going to a meeting to going to school for the purpose of learning, training, and activating other believers for the work of the ministry or their respective areas of influence in the world. When we equip more believers and help them to awaken to their spiritual gifts, we will see more souls converted for the end-time harvest.

Spiritual Gifts
Everyone has been endowed with some sort of spiritual gift to benefit the world and the people in it. Some people come into the knowledge of it and use it for their own self-gratification and pleasures. Some use their gifts to glorify God and bless others. Some have no idea what their gifts are or what they were purposed to do. You will become more aware of your spiritual gifts and have more understanding of your assignment and purpose when God awakens your spiritual senses and activates them. I was one of those who was not aware I had spiritual gifts. This caused me to run down the wrong path and make a lot of mistakes until I hit shipwreck. Sometimes a shipwreck is the best thing that can happen to you if that is what it takes for God to get your attention. I was living a life of sex, partying, and drinking with no

direction for my life. It was in the moment I said yes to God that everything began to change for me. God began to change my perspective of myself, Him, and the world. There are many spiritual gifts, but they are released as God wills by the Holy Spirit and our personal desires. God gives us spiritual gifts to assist with our assignments on Earth.

Gifts in the form of abilities

1 Corinthians 12:4-6 NIV reads, *"There are different kinds of gifts, but the same Spirit distributes them. There are different kinds of service, but the same Lord. There are different kinds of working, but in all of them and in everyone it is the same God at work."* If you continue to read, the Apostle Paul begins to list some of those gifts that are in the form of abilities: words of wisdom, words of knowledge, gift of faith, gifts of healing, miracles, prophecy, discerning of spirits, gift of tongues, and interpretation of tongues.

Gifts in the form of people

Ephesians 4:8 NIV reads, *"This is why it says: 'When he ascended on high, he took many captives and gave gifts to his people."* The Holy Spirit gives everyone their gifts based on our own assignments, purpose, and identity. Some gifts are abilities, but there are other gifts the Apostle

Paul talks about that God has given to the church in the form of ministry leaders. Ephesians 4:11-12 KJV reads, *"And he gave some, apostles; and some, prophets; and some, evangelists; and some, pastors and teachers; for the perfecting of the saints, for the work of the ministry, for the edifying of the body of Christ: till we all come in the unity of the faith, and of the knowledge of the Son of God, unto a perfect man, unto the measure of the stature of the fullness of Christ."* The key word in this passage is "some". So, if some are apostles, prophets, pastors, evangelists, and teachers, what is everyone else? I believe the answer is in 1 Corinthians 12:29 NIV which reads, *"Are all Apostles? Are all Prophets? Are all teachers? Are all workers of miracles? Do all have gifts of healing? Do all speak in tongues? Do all interpret?"* The answer is: no. There are many other gifts (people) in the Body who have other expressions of God which are created to glorify God and bless the Body of Christ. These gifts may come in the form of leading worship, praise dancing, visual art, administration, hospitality, or any of the other many types of ministry expressions.

We are not all the same, we do not all function the same, and we do not all sound the same. God has made everyone unique, but I do believe your personality and spiritual gifts can give you more understanding of your identity, which reveals purpose. Before you mature in the full understanding of your gifts and where you are called to serve, you must understand who you are as a son. The understanding of Sonship and identity will keep everything in the right perspective so we can see God as Father and not just Judge and Ruler. We are not servants; we are sons that serve their father. There is a big difference. Sons receive inheritance and servants do not. Sons know what their father is doing (John 5:19-20 KJV), servants do not know what their master is doing. (John 15:15 KJV) I believe the mistake many of us have made was boxing God only in the church culture. I am guilty of this as well, but I thank God for freedom and growth. The Kingdom of God is a government culture, and God wants to infiltrate every sphere of influence to establish his Kingdom. He cannot do that unless His people know who they are, what they are supposed to do, and where they are supposed to be.

There are seven cultural mountains of influence within the World: religion, family, business, education, media, arts and entertainment, and government. The reason God made everyone different is because He makes everyone acceptable and designed for their assignment. It is also His manifold grace and sovereignty that makes a winner out of anyone and turns any situation around. God wants to reveal His divine diversity in all mankind regardless of race, ethnicity, and culture. I believe some are called to the Body of Christ to train and release others in their respectful places. Others are called to go into the world, but not be of it, and be fruitful, multiply, and replenish the Earth. They are to have dominion in the areas where God has called them to in the name of the Lord (Genesis 1:28). Without an understanding of their identity, they will more than likely settle instead of becoming an influencer for God. They will settle for being an usher, greeter, or elder when God may call them to do much more. There is nothing wrong with any of these positions, but we must be sure we are following God's design for our personal lives. He may be calling you to be a government official, a producer of positive messages in Hollywood producing positive messages through entertainment and media, or making an impact for God in the educational or business world. God did not get anyone saved to just become church members, but to become sons and lead.

My instructions on this lesson are:

1. *Change* the way you see church.

2. *Find* a 5-fold ministry that will teach, train, and develop you as a son.

3. *As you develop* a relationship with the Holy Spirit, begin to ask Him who you are and what you were created to do.

4. *Read and meditate* on the epistles written by the early Apostles so you can embrace your new identity as a son.

5. *Allow God* to connect you to destiny partners who are to help you on the way. Some are temporary and some are forever. Be okay with both.

Pray this Prayer:

Father,
You said in Matthew 7:7 Ask, and it shall be given, seek and I shall find, knock and the door will be opened, so I ask that you reveal to me who I am and what I'm supposed to do. I stand knocking and asking, and I will continue seeking until all is revealed to me in Jesus' name. Holy Spirit, I ask that you reveal these things to me and bring me into all truth in Jesus' name! Amen!

8

UNSHAKEABLE FAITH

Faith in Greek is *pistis*: to be persuaded, to come to trust. In Hebrew faith is *aman*: agreement, firm regulation, fixed provision, a covenant. The word covenant means guarantee, contract, pledge, promise. Hebrews 11:1 KJV reads, *"Now faith is the substance of things hoped for, the evidence of things not seen."* For the believer, faith is a gift, unearned or deserved. It is God's divine persuasion which is distinctly different from human belief (confidence or self-confidence), it is God-confidence. Faith is confidence in Him, what He says, His ability to perform what He says and His power to bring it into existence.

Faith is...
   1. A Gift.
   Ephesians 2:8-9 AMPC reads, *"For it is by free grace (God's unmerited favor) that you are saved ([a]delivered from judgment and made partakers of Christ's salvation) through [your] faith. And this [salvation] is not of yourselves [of your own doing, it came not*

through your own striving], but it is the gift of God; Not because of works [not the fulfillment of the Law's demands], lest any man should boast. [It is not the result of what anyone can possibly do, so no one can pride himself in it or take glory to himself.]"

2. One of the Fruits of the Spirit.
Galatians 5:22-23 AMPC reads, *"But the fruit of the [Holy] Spirit [the work which His presence within accomplishes] is love, joy (gladness), peace, patience (an even temper, forbearance), kindness, goodness (benevolence), faithfulness, gentleness (meekness, humility), self-control (self-restraint, continence). Against such things there is no law [[a]that can bring a charge]."*

3. Our Communication and Connection with God.
Luke 4:4 AMPC reads, *"And Jesus replied to him, it is written, Man shall not live and be sustained by (on) bread alone [b]but by every word and expression of God."* Matthew 4:4 AMPC reads, *"But He replied, It has been written, Man shall not live and be upheld and sustained by bread alone, but by every word that comes forth from the mouth of God."*

Faith is not...

1. Faith is not the same as hope, but it works well with faith. Faith allows us to experience salvation. Hope secures our faith in the complete work of Christ and gives us something to look forward to.

2. Faith is not believing for what we say or want, but what God wants and says for us and to us.

3. Faith is not just required to come to the Kingdom, it is required to live in the Kingdom for God's intended purpose to be manifested. This does not mean God loves you any more or any less. It reveals our level of love and trust toward Him as our Father and provider. Faith is the prerequisite to living a life pleasing to God as well as the currency to unlocking a supernatural power of God in the life of a believer.

4. Faith is not following rules, regulations, or laws. Although it is good to follow all these things, we are not justified by the works of the law but by our faith in Jesus. Faith is being obedient to the Spirit of God when He speaks or leads you to do something.

Galatians 2:16 AMPC reads, *"Yet we know that a man is justified or reckoned righteous and in right standing with God not by works of the Law, but [only] through faith and [absolute] reliance on and adherence to and trust in Jesus Christ (the Messiah, the Anointed One). [Therefore] even we [ourselves] have believed on Christ Jesus, in order to be justified by faith in Christ and not by works of the Law [for we cannot be justified by any observance of the ritual of the Law given by Moses], because by keeping legal rituals and by works no human being can ever be justified (declared righteous and put in right standing.*

Hebrews 11:6 KJV reads, *"But without faith it is impossible to please him: for he that cometh to God must believe that he is, and that he is a rewarder of them that diligently seek him."*

James 2:14 AMPC reads, *"What is the use (profit), my brethren, for anyone to profess to have faith if he has no [good] works [to show for it]? Can [such] faith save [his soul]?"*

Galatians 5:6 AMPC reads, *"For [if we are] in Christ Jesus neither circumcision nor uncircumcision means anything, but only faith activated and expressed and working through love."*

Examples of Faith:

Abel

Hebrews 11:4 AMPC reads, "*[Prompted, actuated] by faith Abel brought God a better and more acceptable sacrifice than Cain, because of which it was testified of him that he was righteous [that he was upright and in right standing with God], and God bore witness by accepting and acknowledging his gifts. And though he died, yet [through the incident] he is still speaking.*"

Enoch

Hebrews 11:5 AMPC reads, "*Because of faith Enoch was caught up and transferred to heaven, so that he did not have a glimpse of death; and he was not found, because God had translated him. For even before he was taken to heaven, he received testimony [still on record] that he had pleased and been satisfactory to God.*"

Noah

Hebrews 11:7 AMPC reads, "*[Prompted] by faith Noah, being forewarned by God concerning events of which as yet there was no visible sign, took heed and diligently and reverently constructed and prepared an ark for the deliverance of his own family. By this [his faith which relied on God] he passed judgment and sentence on the world's unbelief and became an heir and possessor of righteousness ([a]that relation of being right into which God puts the person who has faith)."*

Sarah

Hebrews 11:11 AMPC reads, *"Because of faith also Sarah herself received physical power to conceive a child, even when she was long past the age for it, because she considered [God] Who had given her the promise to be reliable and trustworthy and true to His word."*

Isaac, Jacob, Esau, and Joseph

Hebrews 11:20-22 AMPC reads, *"[With eyes of] faith Isaac, looking far into the future, invoked blessings upon Jacob and Esau. [Prompted] by faith Jacob, when he was dying, blessed each of Joseph's sons and bowed in prayer over the top of his staff. [Actuated] by faith Joseph, when nearing the end of his life, referred to [the promise of God for] the departure of the Israelites out of Egypt and gave instructions concerning the burial of his own bones."*

Rahab

Hebrews 11:31 AMPC reads, *"[Prompted] by faith Rahab the prostitute was not destroyed along with those who refused to believe and obey, because she had received the spies in peace [without enmity]."*

Abraham – The Father of Faith

Hebrews 11:8-10 AMPC reads, *"[Urged on] by faith Abraham, when he was called, obeyed and went forth to a place which he was destined to receive as an inheritance; and he went, although he did not know or trouble his mind about where he was to go. [Prompted] by faith he dwelt as a temporary resident in the land which was designated in the promise [of God, though he was like a stranger] in a strange country, living in tents with Isaac and Jacob, fellow heirs with him of the same promise. For he was [waiting expectantly and confidently] looking forward to the city which has fixed and firm foundations, whose Architect and Builder is God."*

Hebrews 11:17:19 AMPC reads, *"By faith Abraham, when he was put to the test [while the testing of his faith was [a]still in progress], [b]had already brought Isaac for an offering; he who had gladly received and welcomed [God's] promises was ready to sacrifice his only son,18 Of whom it was said, Through Isaac shall your descendants be reckoned.19 For he reasoned that God was able to raise [him] up even from among the dead. Indeed in the sense that Isaac was figuratively dead [potentially sacrificed], he did [actually] receive him back from the dead.*

The Bible refers to Abraham as the "Father of Faith" because of his radical obedience and willingness to believe God for something he could not see. It is interesting to me that although Abraham did not do everything right, he was still justified in the sight of God because of his faith. I believe there are lessons we can take from Abraham's life to learn the reasons God was so pleased with him. God considered Abraham a friend because of his childlike faith and willingness to obey everything he told him. He exercised his faith each time God spoke to him. Abraham was 75 years old when God initially spoke to him, and 99 when he received the promise of his first born through his wife Sarah. That is a total of 24 years Abraham had to wait for his promise without wavering!

Just like many of us, Abraham's wife began to get a little impatient and did not know how God was going to do it, so she asked Abraham to take her servant and have a child with her. Although it was not God's instructions, God still showed mercy and grace toward them both. He was 86 when Hagar, Sarah's servant, bore Ishmael his first born.

Even when Abraham lied about his wife being his sister to King Abimelech in Genesis 20:1-16 out of fear for his life, God never mentioned it to Abraham. He protected them both and never brought it up.

My reason for sharing this story is to help you understand when you decide to live by your faith in Christ like Abraham did, faith is what justifies you as well. Your sins, mistakes, and shortcomings have been taken care of and purified through the blood so God will not bring them up either if you continue to walk by faith. Abraham's obedience and faith made him a father of the faith. Every spiritual blessing released to Abraham has also been released to every believer through faith in Jesus Christ. It is our inheritance as heirs according to the promise he made to Abraham. That is great news! We did not have to earn it or deserve it. It was given to all who believe in Jesus. See Galatians 3:14, 3:29.

This is what I believe will help you build your faith:

1. *Whenever God speaks to you* concerning anything, receive it. Write

it down and meditate on it until you know you believe it. We must train ourselves to become fully persuaded like Abraham, so we are not being paralyzed by fear but energized by our faith.

2. *Spend time in the presence of the Lord* and fellowship with the Holy Spirit. This can be done through prayer, meditation, reading, or even in everyday activities such as exercising, walking, working, driving, or even bathing. God is everywhere, therefore we must acknowledge His presence to be aware He is present.

3. *Learn to include God* in every decision you make. This can seem a little extreme, but the blessing in the discipline of this and wisdom the Holy Spirit will release will safeguard you in times to come. The Holy Spirit desires to speak to you so keep the lines of communication open.

4. *Practice your faith* by applying practically everything you say you believe spiritually. Revisit this sentence. Faith without works is dead. Our faith is

not activated until we apply the spiritual principles we learn.

5. *Extra Study:* 2 Corinthians 4:18, Matthew 4:4, and Psalms 119:105.

<u>*Pray this Prayer:*</u>

Father,
I thank you for unshakable faith, unwavering faith, uncompromising faith. I thank you for childlike faith where when you say something, I believe it and take you at your word. Just as Abraham considered not his natural body, I consider not my natural circumstances. I focus not on the things that are seen but the things that are unseen. Your word declares that man shall not live by bread alone but by every word that proceeds out of your mouth. I thank you father for allowing your word to be a lamp to my feet and light to my path In Jesus name. May faith be perfected in me.
Amen.

9

PRAYER: STAYING CONNECTED TO THE POWER SOURCE

Prayer can simply be defined as talking to God, but that is just how the relationship begins. It is often used as a communication or channel for God to connect Heaven and Earth. As we pray, God can get things accomplished and released because of our agreement to partner with heaven. Our prayer levels and dimensions change as our relationship and intimacy grows with the Lord. According to Derrick Prince's *"Secrets of a Prayer Warrior,"* there are 12 types of prayers: Synergy, Thanksgiving and Praise, Worship, Petitions, Intercession, Supplication, Command, Commitment, Dedication, Persistence, Blessing, and Cursing. Learning the principles of prayer could make a difference in having an effective prayer life. I will touch briefly on just a few principles, but I encourage you to purchase this book.

Synergy

The foundational text for this type of prayer is in Matthew 18:19-20, which in the New King James Version reads, *"Again I say to you that if two of you agree to anything on earth concerning anything that they ask, it will be done for them by my father in Heaven. For where two or three are gathered together in my name, I am in the midst of them."* Synergy is the power of agreement and unity with others and God in prayer. The Holy Spirit orchestrates the harmony of bringing people together for the sake of prayer and releasing the will of the Father in the lives of His people.

Example: *Father, you said in Matthew 18:19-20, if we touch and agree to anything we ask in your name that you would do it so even we thank you for healing _____ and we thank your opening new doors and opportunities for _____ to receive a new job, new business, new resources in the name of Jesus, and by faith we believe they receive it according to Mark 11:24 and 1 John 5:14-15 in Jesus name! Amen.*

Thanksgiving and Praise

Psalms 100:4 KJV reads, *"Enter into his gates with thanksgiving, and into his courts with praise: be thankful unto him and bless his name."*

This scripture describes the attitude we are to enter the presence of Lord with. We must be grateful, humble, and willing to acknowledge His goodness through kind words that exalt His name, character, and nature.

Example: Father, I thank you for giving me every spiritual blessing in Christ Jesus. I thank you for giving me everything pertaining to life and godliness in the knowledge of you. I thank you for enlightening the eyes of my understanding that I may know the height, length, and depths of your love for me. You are mighty, awesome, and powerful. You are our healer and deliver. Father, you are the King of Kings and Lord of Lords and before you there is no other.

Petition and Supplication

Prayer is not only our communication with God, but it is also a way we commune with God. It is where He shares and exchanges intimate thoughts and feelings concerning us. Prayer is our very source of connection to Him. I call it our power source because God can make divine transfers into our spirit and soul in prayer. He imparts into our spirit while transferring our hurt and pain for comfort and healing, our grief and sorrow for joy and strength, and fear for peace and love. The Father deposits whatever we need by way of prayer and spending time in His presence. We are encouraged in scriptures to not worry about anything and pray about everything. In Philippians 4:6 and Luke 9-13, we are taught how petition and supplication works. To petition means to present your request and to be specific in prayer. To make supplication is the act of asking or begging for something earnestly, meaning to apply persistence. Petition and supplication produce the most results when we exercise consistency and remain persistent in prayer. Despite how bad it looks or feels, we must be willing to stand on the promises of God that are in His word. This prayer will require a person to activate their faith and magnify the promise over any problem they face.

Prayer was a source of strength for Jesus during His time on the Earth. He prayed before assignments, after He completed assignments, to receive direction from the Father, and even when He was unsettled about what He would have to endure to get to the Cross. In the Garden of Gethsemane, Jesus was so troubled He began to sweat drops of blood because of the anguish He felt. Even in His anguish, He was willing to die to Himself to please the Father. Prayer was a major source of strength for Him in this moment. When we are weak God sends angels to minister to us just as He did with Jesus in this moment. Luke 22:41-43 KJV reads, *"And he withdrew about a stone's throw beyond them, where he knelt down and prayed, "Father, if you are willing, take this cup from me. Yet not my will but yours be done." Then an Angel from heaven appeared to him and strengthened him. And in his anguish, he prayed more earnestly, and his sweat became like drops of blood falling to the ground. When Jesus rose from prayer and returned to the disciples, he found them asleep, exhausted from sorrow. "Why are you sleeping?" He asked. Get up and pray so that you will not enter into temptation."* While Jesus prayed, the disciples slept. This is the reason Peter failed under temptation and denied Him because he was not found praying to be strengthened, endure and stand persecution, and accusations. He later learned this principle and he never denied Jesus again.

As believers, our prayer life will be the determining factor about a lot of things in our existence. Whether we are maturing or not, overcoming or falling short, completing our God-given assignments, or just sitting in church on Sundays. It is not the will of God for us to do the things of God without getting to know Him intimately and becoming more acquainted with His ways. Be clear. God desires for us to partner with Him in releasing Heaven on Earth, which is the reason everyone is called to be an intercessor in some capacity. Jesus is at the right-hand interceding for us. The Holy Spirit makes intercession for us, and God assigns people to intercede for us. Intercession is the act of praying on the behalf of others, while showing adoration toward the Father. In doing this, we open ourselves up for worship by giving ourselves to the Lord for the sake of His Kingdom and purpose. In John 4:23, Jesus speaks on how God is looking for true worshippers that will worship Him in spirit and truth, not just pray when they need Him to do something. Worship is when you love Him through praise, admiration, for who He is to you, and what He has already done.

10

LIVING IN THE SPIRIT

Living in the Spirit is a process that takes time, but it is the ultimate goal to walk in maturity. Before you can walk in the Spirit, you first must be Spirit-filled and Spirit-driven with an understanding of the Word. To be Spirit-filled is to have your impulses yielded to the Holy Spirit where you can produce more of the fruits of the Spirit than of the flesh. Being filled with the Spirit produces fruit of righteousness and holiness such as: love, joy, peace, patience, self-control, kindness, goodness, faithfulness, and gentleness. There is a process of sanctification and consecration that happens before the fruits are cultivated and manifested.

To be spiritually driven, means to be consciously aware and sensitive to the spirit of God in you. Additionally, you are aware of your own spirit, which God uses to guide you and communicate to you. It means you do not desire to move, speak, or do anything without His leading. We see an example of this in John 5:19 when Jesus said, *"I only speak and do what I see my father doing."* We also see it with Moses in Exodus 33:15 when he declares if God's presence did not go with them, he would not want to go or lead the people. Moses was Spirit-driven. Living in the Spirit is when you embrace all three: being full of the Spirit, spiritually sensitive to God, and full of the Word of God. It is out of that revelation which you live and speak.

Living in the Spirit requires keen sensitivity to the Holy Spirit where you would consider Him and His feelings before doing things and speaking. This is the place of maturity where Jesus operated. Jesus knew the Word and the voice of the Father, so if He heard anything to the contrary, He was able to stand and resist attacks, tricks, and fiery darts. Despite common beliefs, I believe it is attainable but requires being intentional, disciplined, and sold out for God. As long as there are parts of us that desire other things that are not in alignment with the timing and purpose of God, it will be difficult. God has a plan to perfect those things concerning us, but we must fix our eyes on Jesus who is the author and finisher of our faith.

Psalms 138:8 ESV reads, *"The Lord will fulfill his*

purpose for me; your steadfast love, O Lord, endures forever. Do not forsake the work of your hands."

Hebrews 12:2 KJV reads, *"Looking unto Jesus the author and finisher of our faith, who for the joy that was set before him endured the cross, despising the shame, and is set down at the right hand of the throne of God."*

Colossians 1:10 NIV reads, *"...so that you may live a life worthy of the Lord and please him in every way: bearing fruit in every good work, growing in the knowledge of God..."*

Ephesians 4:30 NIV reads, *"And do not grieve the Holy Spirit of God, with whom you were sealed for the day of redemption."*

Pray this Prayer:

Father,

I thank you for filling me and baptizing with your Holy Spirit. Help me to be engulfed into the life of the Spirit, the mind of the Spirit, and desires of the Spirit, that I may live a life pleasing to Him, that I may not grieve or vex Him but help me to be sensitive to the Holy Spirit and be led by Him in all my ways. In Jesus' name! Amen.

11

EMBRACING A KINGDOM PERSPECTIVE

Imagine a culture where everyone saw one another the way God sees them, called them what God calls them, and respected one another as God intended. What was the purpose of the Ten Commandments, and the new command Jesus gave for us to love one another as He has loved us? The purpose of the Ten Commandments was to show God's people how far they were from Him. God knew they could not keep the law, so He established principles for us to live by instead. Some of the principles Jesus taught through the parables were the importance of humility, love, forgiveness, mercy, grace, honor, compassion, and the law of sowing and reaping. It requires humility to be pure in heart. It requires a pure heart to fulfill His commandment to love one another and honor those in authority, as well as our brothers and sisters in Christ. This is what it means to be a peacemaker. It requires compassion to be merciful toward others. Jesus desired to please God over man.

We live in a world that has created a culture opposite of everything I just shared. God wants His sons and daughters to create a Kingdom culture, where every relationship reflects our relationship with God. A culture where we are careful to reflect the heart of the Father in how we see people, talk to people, and treat them so that He may reach them through us. The world is selfish-driven, and everyone is concerned only about themselves. The danger is we receive a return of whatever seeds we sow. So, we should be sure to sow good to please our Father in Heaven.

Galatians 6:7 KJV reads, *"Be not deceived God is not mocked, for whatsoever a man soweth, that he shall also reap."*

Matthew 7:12 NIV reads, *"So in everything, do to others what you would have them do to you, for this sums up the Law and the Prophets."*

Romans 12:10 NIV reads, *"Be devoted to one another in love. Honor one another above yourselves."*

Ephesians 5:21 NKJV reads, *"...Submitting yourselves one to another in the fear of God."*

Hebrews 13:1-3 NIV reads, *"Keep on loving one another as brothers and sisters. Do not forget to show hospitality to strangers, for by so doing some people have shown hospitality to angels without knowing it. Continue to remember those in prison as if you were together with them in prison, and those who are mistreated as if you yourselves were suffering."*

Romans 12:3 NIV reads, *"For by the grace given me I say to every one of you: Do not think of yourself more highly than you ought, but rather think of yourself with sober judgment, in accordance with the faith God has distributed to each of you."*

Philippians 2:3 NIV reads, *"Do nothing out of selfish ambition or vain conceit. Rather, in humility value others above yourselves..."*

Fellow believers, we are to submit to one another in the fear of the Lord, to be considerate and understanding to one another. To submit means to accept or yield to a superior force or authority of another person. We are to carry each other's burdens and be there for one another. We are even to be kind to strangers and people we do not know according to the Word.

In conclusion, I believe what God is really looking for is a diverse family who loves and honors Him in everything. He desires for us to demonstrate that love and honor through our relationship with others. When we embrace this revelation and begin to live this way, then we will be able to truly walk as children of the light. This understanding allows us to take responsibility for our part of making a difference in the world by expressing the Kingdom of Heaven within us and releasing it around us. It is sad enough that sometimes it is the people who do not know Jesus who are the most genuine. Man judges according to flesh, but God looks at the heart. We must always make sure our hearts and intentions are pure concerning others and know our reward comes from Heaven.

The Parable of the Good Samaritan

Luke 10:25-37 NIV reads, *"On one occasion an expert in the law stood up to test Jesus. "Teacher," he asked, "what must I do to inherit eternal life?" What is written in the Law?" he replied. "How do you read it?" He answered, "'Love the Lord your God with all your heart and with all your soul and with all your strength and with all your mind'[a]; and 'Love your neighbor as yourself.'[b]" "You have answered correctly," Jesus replied. "Do this and you will live." But he wanted to justify himself, so he asked Jesus, "And who is my neighbor?" In reply Jesus said: "A man was going down from Jerusalem to Jericho, when he was attacked by robbers. They stripped him of his clothes, beat him and went away, leaving him half dead. A priest happened to be going down the same road, and when he saw the man, he passed by on the other side. So too, a Levite, when he came to the place and saw him, passed by on the other side. But a Samaritan, as he traveled, came where the man was; and when he saw him, he took pity on him. He went to him and bandaged his wounds, pouring on oil and wine. Then he put the man on his own donkey, brought him to an inn and took care of him. The next day he took out two denarii[c] and gave them to the innkeeper. 'Look after him,' he said, 'and when I return, I will reimburse you for any extra expense you may have.' "Which of these three do you think was a neighbor to the man who fell into the hands of robbers?" The expert in the law replied, "The one who had mercy on him." Jesus told him, "Go and do likewise."*

According to the parable, your neighbor is anyone that needs help whether you know them or not. Jesus was making a strong statement by showing two different religious leaders that totally ignored the needs of the man and kept walking. He went even further by using the Example of the good Samaritan that had mercy upon the man that was beaten and robbed. Jesus was showing them that the church alone will not justify or save them. What they think they know about God will not save them, and what they do for God will not save them if they fail to obey the greatest commandment,

"Love your neighbor as yourself. "Then he tells them to go and do likewise. Jesus always addresses the center of the heart, the motive and intention of the individual.

12

UNITY, THE POWER OF ONE

Confusion in The Church

I often wonder if we, the Church, understood the power of unity, would we still argue, debate, and divide ourselves because of so many things we disagree about. The truth is you do not have to agree with anyone to love them. Finding a way to navigate through those differences may be difficult without the guidance and wisdom of the Holy Spirit, however it's definitely possible. I believe sometimes He will lead you to separate from others because they have no intention of changing, so in order to protect you and your influence, He will have you to separate from others to avoid disunity through religious and carnal minded people and systems. There can only be unity where there is agreement and commitment.

In Genesis 11:1- 9, we see a people come together who did not know God, who did not love each other or agree on everything, but because they all had the same common goal which was to build a tower that would reach to Heaven, they unified. In this biblical historical story, we see God come down to see what they were doing. He said something that immediately caught attention because none of these people lived for Him. He said, *"These men are all one and they have one language and speak the same thing, nothing they have imagined shall be restrained from them."* Notice God did not reference that they were sinners trying to do this, He only spoke of their faith and unity. He said because they were one, unified in agreement spiritually, physically, mentally, and verbally concerning building this tower, nothing they have imagined will be impossible for them. I like to call this the power of unity. These men were in agreement and committed to the vision presented to them and were willing to work together to see it through. The Lord had to come down and confuse their languages in order to stop them naturally because they were one in the spirit. After He changed their languages, they could not understand one another. Therefore, they were unable to complete the assignment.

Now that we have a bit of an understanding the power unity can produce, how can we bring it into modern day civilization and the church to see change around us? Well, I believe the Body of Christ plays a particularly important role in impacting culture, but it begins with the church coming to true repentance and divine alignment according to His will and purpose for the Bride of Christ. The Body of Christ has always been divided into denominations and religious sectors: Baptist, Pentecostal, Methodism, Catholicism, Angelic, Lutheran, Presbyterian, Protestantism, Church of God in Christ, Evangelical, Assembly of God, Non-Denomination, and so many others. The first issue with this is that it divides us as a body. The foundation, theology, and beliefs are not all the same. The teachings are not the same, so they do not produce the same results. The second issue is theology is the study of God and scripture according to man's interpretation and understanding. This is an issue because neither God nor scripture can be effectively interpreted without the gift of the Holy Spirit. God is a spirit and the words that were written were spiritually inspired. It was never God's intent for man to create doctrine and religion based on man's interpretation *without* the Holy Spirit. The Holy Spirit opens the eyes of our understanding to scripture, and helps us to connect with God. Without Him, it is impossible. God is a spirit. To communicate with Him and understand His communication to us, we must be born-again and receive His spirit. Jesus provided a way for this to be done, but every doctrine does not teach it. The devil has had the church blind for centuries. He is known as the prince of this world over the Kingdom of Darkness according to the Bible. Ephesians 2:2 Amp states, "In which you once walked. You were following the ways of this world [influenced by this present age], in accordance with the prince of the power of the air (Satan), the spirit who is now at work in the disobedient [the unbelieving, who fight against the purposes of God]."

He is known as the prince of darkness (ignorance), and he uses that to his advantage. That way, the church remains powerless because a house divided against itself cannot stand. If the body of Christ is going to be effective, we must become one. We must be willing to drop our religion and pick up the Kingdom mandate. Jesus did not come talking about any of those denominations, only about the message and reality of God's kingdom that was to come on the Earth. Jesus' parables were to be spiritually discerned, not intellectually understood. The Holy Spirit gives us the understanding in our spirit and our spirit translates it to our mind. Trying to comprehend God and His word without His spirit will always lead to error and deception. Satan is known as the father of lies, so he is totally fine with Christians going to church and not changing or changing anything around them.

Matthew 12:22-28 NKJV reads, *"Then one was brought to Him who was demon-possessed, blind and mute; and He healed him, so that the [a]blind and mute man both spoke and saw. And all the multitudes were amazed and said, "Could this be the Son of David?" Now when the Pharisees heard it they said, "This fellow does not cast out demons except by [b]Beelzebub, the ruler of the demons." But Jesus knew their thoughts, and said to them: "Every kingdom divided against itself is brought to desolation, and every city or house divided against itself will not stand. If Satan casts out Satan, he is divided against himself. How then will his kingdom stand? And if I cast out demons by Beelzebub, by whom do your sons cast them out? Therefore they shall be your judges. But if I cast out demons by the Spirit of God, surely the kingdom of God has come upon you."*

John 4:24 KJV reads, *"God is a Spirit: and they that worship him must worship him in spirit and in truth."*

John 6:63 NIV reads, *"The Spirit gives life; the flesh counts for nothing. The words I have spoken to you – they are full of the Spirit and life.*

John 16:13 NKJV reads, *"However, when He, the Spirit of truth, has come, He will guide you into all truth; for He will not speak on His own authority, but whatever He hears He will speak; and He will tell you things to come."*

Aligning The Body

To align something, we must be aware there is an issue. For instance, when you drive your car, over time you will notice your wheels are out of alignment by the sway of your steering wheel to the left or to the right. The swaying informs you that it is time to schedule your car for an alignment and tire rotation. In the same way a car needs an alignment, the Body of Christ needs to be brought to the Master for the church to be put into divine alignment. For years, churches have been trying to make it with just the pastor, bishop, usher, and so on. Unless the foundation is fixed, we will continue out of tradition and religion. According to scripture, the foundation of the church was founded upon First the Apostles, then the prophets and third the teachers with Christ being the cornerstone.

Ephesians 2:20 New Revised Standard Version: "built upon the foundation of the apostles and prophets, with Christ Jesus himself as the cornerstone. [a]"

1 Corinthians 12:28 AMP: So God has appointed and placed in the church [for His own use]: first apostles [chosen by Christ], second prophets [those who foretell the future, those who speak a new message from God to the people], third teachers, then those who work miracles, then those with the gifts of healings, the helpers, the administrators, and speakers in various kinds of [unknown] tongues."

Why is this important? We have many parts as the Body of Christ, which means we have many administrations, abilities, and gifts particularly for God, but specifically to connect others to the purposes of God. Everyone gets to play their part, but when the foundation is not right, we have people just gathering out of convenience instead of purpose. The purpose of the church is to introduce people to God through Christ then build, train, equip, and release disciples to fulfill the "Great Commission" by going into all the world to make an impact. Just as the disciples in the Book of Acts. God's purpose did not change, the church's focus did. Some churches would rather put on concerts, conferences, and programs that do not change the people involved. There is nothing wrong with any of these things, but why should we have to go to conferences to get training when our local churches should be able to do it? This is the reason we must follow the order God established in the Body of Christ.

According to 1 Corinthians 12:28, He set first apostles, second prophets, and third teachers. There is no level of importance, it simply establishes the order of responsibility. In the same way He created Adam first and placed him as the head over Eve, this is the order of responsibility He has set for the church. These three play a major part in building a strong foundation in the life of any believer. Apostles, also known as ambassadors for Christ, are sent to represent the Kingdom of God and speak on behalf of Heaven. They are pioneers because God may send them to start a work, plant a church, or help equip a people. Apostles are not raised and sent out by men, only by God to fulfill the Great Commission. Apostles see through an Apostolic perspective and vision as God has given them the blueprint to build the Kingdom wherever the Lord leads.

Prophets are needed. They are considered friends of God because of their closeness to Him. They are lovers of His presence and oftentimes carry a heavy weight of His glory to be able to shift environments and atmospheres because of their authority and sensitivity to the Spirit. Prophets are spokespersons for God. They speak by inspiration on behalf of God to communicate the heart, mind, and purposes of God to people. Prophets hold a governmental position like apostles as their duty is to always point you back to Christ and be able to communicate what God is doing and saying at all times. Prophets give direction, revelation, impartation, information, and confirmation to everyone. They can help steer the boat in the right direction as the Apostle leads so they stay in the will and purpose of God and continue to progress. Apostles, because they are visionary by nature, can miss small details that prophets can bring awareness to. Apostles keep prophets accountable and level-headed to give them a level of balance because they can often choose to be isolated and misunderstood; they need one another to build. The apostolic has to do with being sent, and the prophetic has to do with being in tune with the Holy Spirit. It makes sense God would choose to build His foundation on them. We are all apostolic in the sense that we are sent from God to do a work and prophetic because we do and say what God says. Apostles and prophets are not stationary gifts; therefore, we see the Apostle Paul traveling, planting churches, and building them before moving to the next city. This is how the move of God was able to impact so many people. After the foundation was set, apostles and prophets were then assigned pastors and teachers to help build and train the disciples.

Teachers are especially important to the development of the believer. They teach the Body foundational truths and principles to give them understanding of scripture and the will of God. Pastors probably have one of the hardest jobs because they are called to shepherd the believer, which requires them to nurture, teach, counsel, and labor with the people. God sends help; this is the reason it is important to know our identity so we can benefit the Body.

Evangelists are not stationary gifts either. They are soul conscious. As they get the souls saved and brought into the Body of Christ, everyone else must step in and do their part. Helpers, administrations, dance teams, psalmists, ushers, greeters, etc. all had a part with allowing the Body to function the way it was intended. If we are going to change the world for Christ, the five-fold blueprint must be restored in the body of Christ.

Unity in The Body

Unity in the Body of Christ has to do with many things. The first thing is submitting to God through His word and submitting to one another by creating a culture of love, honor, respect, mercy, forgiveness, and faith. The Bible teaches us to do all things as unto God. The next thing would be embracing a culture of community and family among believers as they did in the first church in the Book of Acts. To create such a culture, the church must be more spiritual and less carnal, by not giving place to competition, jealousy, division, witchcraft, fornication, or any of the works of the flesh Apostle Paul addresses in Galatians 5:19. When you sow from the flesh, you reap to the flesh.

As everyone in the Body of Christ embraces their identity and authenticity, we will experience the manifold grace of God like never before. There are many members in the body with a diversity of gifts and functionality. All parts of the Body are needed in full to experience the best results. Every part is just as important and must be embraced and accepted as such. Different parts and gifts bring a different expression of God. He reveals Himself in ways we could not perceive or comprehend in our own abilities.

Colossians 3:17 NLT reads, *"And whatever you do or say, do it as a representative of the Lord Jesus, giving thanks through him to God the Father."*

Colossians 3:23 NLT reads, *"Work willingly at whatever you do, as though you were working for the Lord rather than for people."*

Acts 2:46 NIV reads, *"Every day they continued to meet together in the temple courts. They broke bread in their homes and ate together with glad and sincere hearts..."*

Romans 12:4-5 NIV reads, *"For just as each of us has one body with many members, and these members do not all have the same function, so in Christ we, though many, form one body, and each member belongs to all the others."*

One Body but Many Parts

1 Corinthians 12:12-27 NIRV reads, *"There is one body, but it has many parts. But all its many parts make up one body. It is the same with Christ. We were all baptized by one Holy Spirit. And so we are formed into one body. It didn't matter whether we were Jews or Gentiles, slaves or free people. We were all given the same Spirit to drink. So the body is not made up of just one part. It has many parts. Suppose the foot says, "I am not a hand. So I don't belong to the body." By saying this, it cannot*

*stop being part of the body. And suppose the ear says,
"I am not an eye. So I don't belong to the body." By
saying this, it cannot stop being part of the body. If
the whole body were an eye, how could it hear? If the
whole body were an ear, how could it smell? God has
placed each part in the body just as he wanted it to
be. If all the parts were the same, how could there be
a body? As it is, there are many parts. But there is
only one body. The eye can't say to the hand, "I don't
need you!" The head can't say to the feet, "I don't
need you!" In fact, it is just the opposite. The parts
of the body that seem to be weaker are the ones we
can't do without. The parts that we think are less
important we treat with special honor. The private
parts aren't shown. But they are treated with special
care. The parts that can be shown don't need special
care. But God has put together all the parts of the
body. And he has given more honor to the parts that
didn't have any. In that way, the parts of the body
will not take sides. All of them will take care of one
another. If one part suffers, every part suffers with it.
If one part is honored, every part shares in its joy.
You are the body of Christ. Each one of you is a part
of it."*

My prayer is for the church to be
awakened to the wisdom and revelation of the
Kingdom to work together to bring more souls
to Christ. I pray everyone can work side by side
to build, teach, and equip other believers for the
work of the ministry. One of the saddest things

is to have a believer who is more concerned about church attendance than they are concerned with making time to pray and spend time with God. Or a believer who cannot articulate what they believe to share with others and defend their faith if need be. If we are going to see Heaven manifested on the Earth, we must learn to pray Heaven to Earth and not Earth to Heaven. By doing this, we are releasing Heaven into the Earth by partnering with God to get His will done.

Pray this Prayer:

Heavenly Father,
I thank you for enlightening the eyes of my understanding. I thank you for allowing me to see who I am in the Body and what I am created to do. I thank you for releasing wisdom unto me and every spiritual gift and blessing in me. I ask you to activate every gift right now in the name of Jesus. I thank you for giving me Kingdom community and family and sending those who have a love for you, for your Word, and for people. I thank you for flooding our eyes with light that we may walk in the knowledge and revelation of your Word. I thank you for unity in the Body of Christ, in our local church, in our global church, in our families, and in our communities. May Heaven come on Earth and through the Body of Christ as it is in Heaven. In Jesus' name, Amen.

About the Author

Eric T. Roscoe is an Apostolic Leader, Kingdom Strategist, Certified-Life Coach, and Business Leader who operates in revelation and impartation.

His teaching empowers the Body of Christ to see the hidden truths of scripture clearly and apply it for everyday results. Eric is the founder of Labor of Love, a ministry that demonstrates the heart and mind of God. He is also the host of the "Build Your Life" weekly podcast. With a heart to see God's Kingdom demonstrated in everyday living, Eric's goal is to inspire everyday people to build their life on God's terms.

Eric has three children and resides in the beautiful Lake Charles, Louisiana.

www.ingramcontent.com/pod-product-compliance
Lightning Source LLC
Chambersburg PA
CBHW052158090426
42741CB00010B/2323